WHAT PEOPLE DO

Curriculum Consultants

Dr. Arnold L. Willems
Associate Professor of Curriculum and Instruction
The University of Wyoming

Dr. Gerald W. Thompson
Associate Professor
Social Studies Education
Old Dominion University

Dr. Dale Rice
Associate Professor
Department of Elementary and Early Childhood Education
University of South Alabama

Dr. Fred Finley
Assistant Professor of Science Education
University of Wisconsin

Subject Area Consultants

Astronomy
Robert Burnham
Associate Editor
Astronomy Magazine and *Odyssey* Magazine

Geology
Dr. Norman P. Lasca
Professor of Geology
University of Wisconsin — Milwaukee

Oceanography
William MacLeish
Editor
Oceanus Magazine

Paleontology
Linda West
Dinosaur National Monument
Jensen, Utah

Physiology
Kirk Hogan, M.D.
Madison, Wisconsin

Sociology/Anthropology
Dr. Arnold Willems
Associate Professor of Curriculum and Instruction
College of Education
University of Wyoming

Technology
Dr. Robert T. Balmer
Professor of Mechanical Engineering
University of Wisconsin — Milwaukee

Transportation
James A. Knowles
Division of Transportation
Smithsonian Institution

Irving Birnbaum
Air and Space Museum
Smithsonian Institution

Donald Berkebile
Division of Transportation
Smithsonian Institution

Zoology
Dr. Carroll R. Norden
Professor of Zoology
University of Wisconsin —
     Milwaukee

First published in Great Britain by Macmillan Children's
   Books, a division of Macmillan Publishers Ltd, under the
   title *Look It Up.*
First edition copyright © 1979, 1981 Macmillan Publishers Ltd
   (for volumes 1-10)
First edition copyright © 1980, 1981 Macmillan Publishers Ltd
   (for volumes 11-16)
Second edition copyright © 1985, 1986 Macmillan Publishers Ltd

Published in the United States of America

Text this edition copyright © 1986 Raintree Publishers Inc.

Library of Congress Number: 86-563

   2 3 4 5 6 7 8 9 0   90 89 88

Printed and bound in the United States of America.

Library of Congress Cataloging-in-Publication Data

Let's discover what people do.

   (Let's discover; 8)
   Bibliography: p. 67
   Includes index.
   Summary: A reference book dealing with the many ways
people earn a living.
   1. Vocational guidance—Juvenile literature.
2. Occupations—Juvenile literature. [1. Occupations.
2. Vocational guidance] I. Title: What people do. II. Series.
AG6.L43   vol. 8, 1986   [HF5381.2]   031s [331.3'1]   86-563
ISBN 0-8172-2607-9 (lib. bdg.)
ISBN 0-8172-2588-9 (softcover)

LET'S DISCOVER

WHAT PEOPLE DO

RAINTREE PUBLISHERS
Milwaukee

Contents

WORKING IN SHOPS _____ **6**

    The baker _____ **8**

    The hairdresser _____ **10**

    The shoemaker _____ **11**

    The supermarket _____ **12**

WORKING ON THE LAND _____ **14**

    Animal farming _____ **16**

    Crop farming _____ **18**

    Gardening _____ **20**

    Working with trees _____ **21**

WORKING AT SEA _____ **22**

    Fishers _____ **24**

    The merchant marine _____ **26**

    The coast guard _____ **28**

    Working on an oil rig _____ **29**

BUILDING AND CONSTRUCTION _____ **30**

    The building site _____ **32**

    Engineers _____ **34**

FACTORIES AND OFFICES _____ **36**

    Working in a factory _____ **36**

    The assembly line _____ **38**

Working with clothes _____ 40

Working in an office _____ 42

SERVICES _____ **44**

Police officers _____ 46

Fire fighters _____ 48

Postal service _____ 50

Trash collectors _____ 51

Teachers _____ 52

Librarians _____ 53

Working in a hospital _____ 54

Doctors _____ 56

Nurses _____ 57

Scientists _____ 58

Working with money _____ 60

Working on a newspaper _____ 62

GLOSSARY _____ **64**

FURTHER READING _____ **67**

QUESTIONS TO THINK ABOUT _____ **69**

PROJECTS _____ **76**

INDEX _____ **77**

WORKING IN SHOPS

This picture shows a shopping area. There are many different kinds of stores and shops. People can go from store to store to buy many different kinds of things. How many kinds of stores and shops can you see?

The baker sells bread, cakes, and cookies. The butcher is standing outside his shop. He sells meat. The supermarket sells foods of all kinds.

The baker

Today, most bread is made in factories and then taken to stores. Some bakers still make their own bread. You can buy fresh bread at these bakeries. It is sometimes still warm from the oven.

First the baker mixes the dough. He uses flour, water, and yeast. Yeast makes the bread rise. Without yeast, the bread would be flat.

When the dough has been mixed, the baker works it with his hands. He turns the dough over and over, folding and pushing it.

The baker shapes the loaves before baking them. Bread can be made into big or small loaves of different shapes.

The shaped loaves are set aside to rise. When they are the right size, the baker puts them into an oven. The hot oven bakes them.

When the bread is baked, the baker takes it out of the oven. He leaves it to cool for a while. Then he takes it into the shop to sell it.

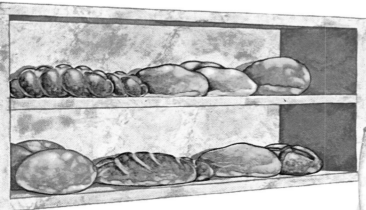

People can choose from many different kinds of bread at a bakery. They can buy white or brown bread. Some bakeries also sell cakes, cookies, and other baked things.

The hairdresser

Hairdressers work in shops called salons. People go to a salon to have their hair cut, washed, or set. Sometimes they ask the hairdresser to give them a new hair style. Some salons have departments for men and women. Shops for men only are called barbers.

The hairdresser starts by washing the customer's hair with shampoo.

Hairdressers can also dye people's hair a different color. This hairdresser is putting on dye with a brush.

Hairdressers usually cut hair while it is still wet.

Some people like their hair curled. The hairdresser winds the wet hair around curlers.

Some people change their hair color by themselves. Warriors in some parts of Africa dye their hair with red clay.

The hairdresser uses a hot air blower to dry the customer's hair. This takes a long time.

The shoemaker

Very few shoemakers make their own shoes. Most shoes today are made in factories. Shoemakers mend shoes. They put on new soles and heels when they wear out.

This shoemaker is putting on new heels. Heels are pounded on with nails.

Some shoemakers use special machines to mend shoes. This makes the work go faster.

The supermarket

In many stores, the owner or the owner's helpers wait on you. In a supermarket, you serve yourself and pay for everything at the checkout counter. In large supermarkets, you can buy food, clothes, books, and many other things.

parking lot

checkout

information

automatic doors

restaurant

main entrance

shopping carts

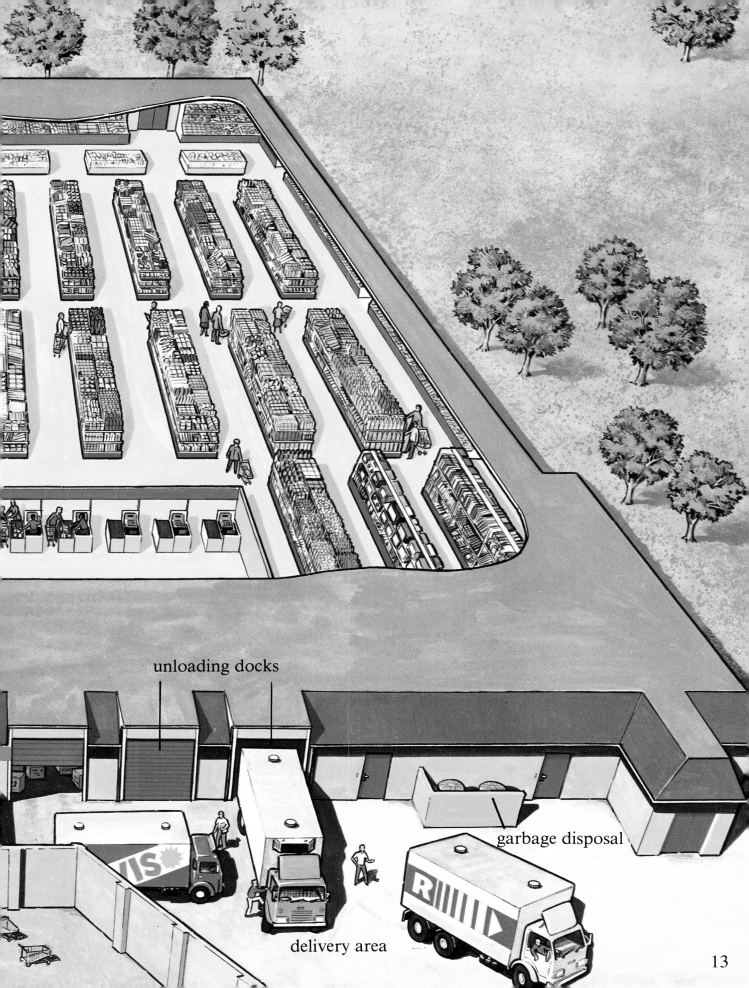

unloading docks

garbage disposal

delivery area

13

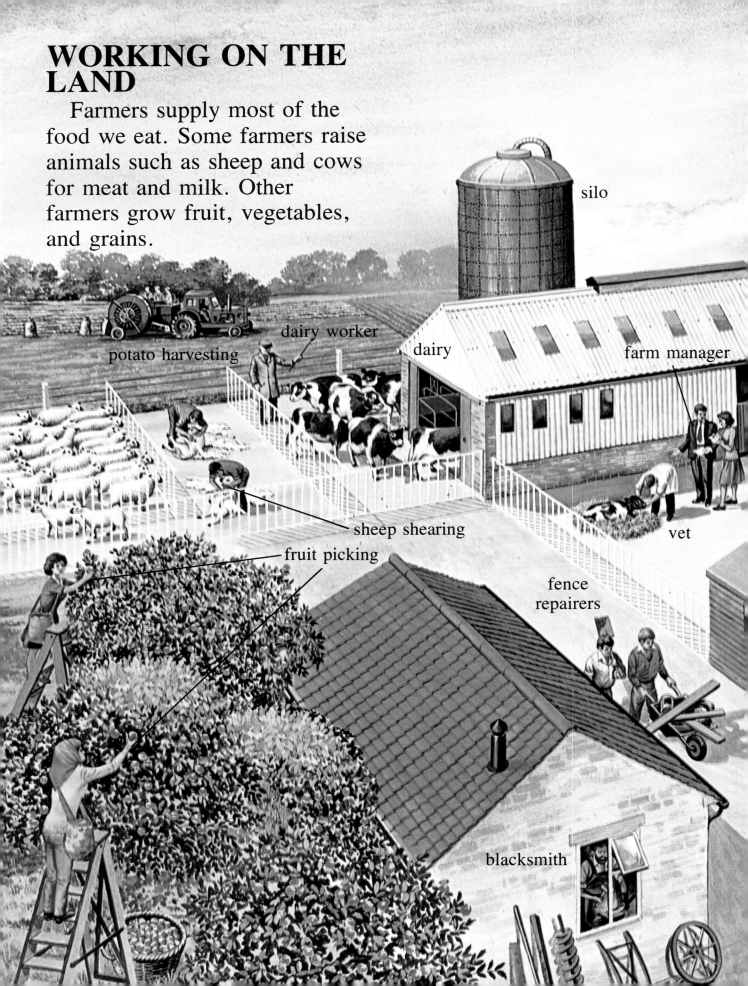

WORKING ON THE LAND

Farmers supply most of the food we eat. Some farmers raise animals such as sheep and cows for meat and milk. Other farmers grow fruit, vegetables, and grains.

silo

potato harvesting

dairy worker

dairy

farm manager

sheep shearing

fruit picking

vet

fence repairers

blacksmith

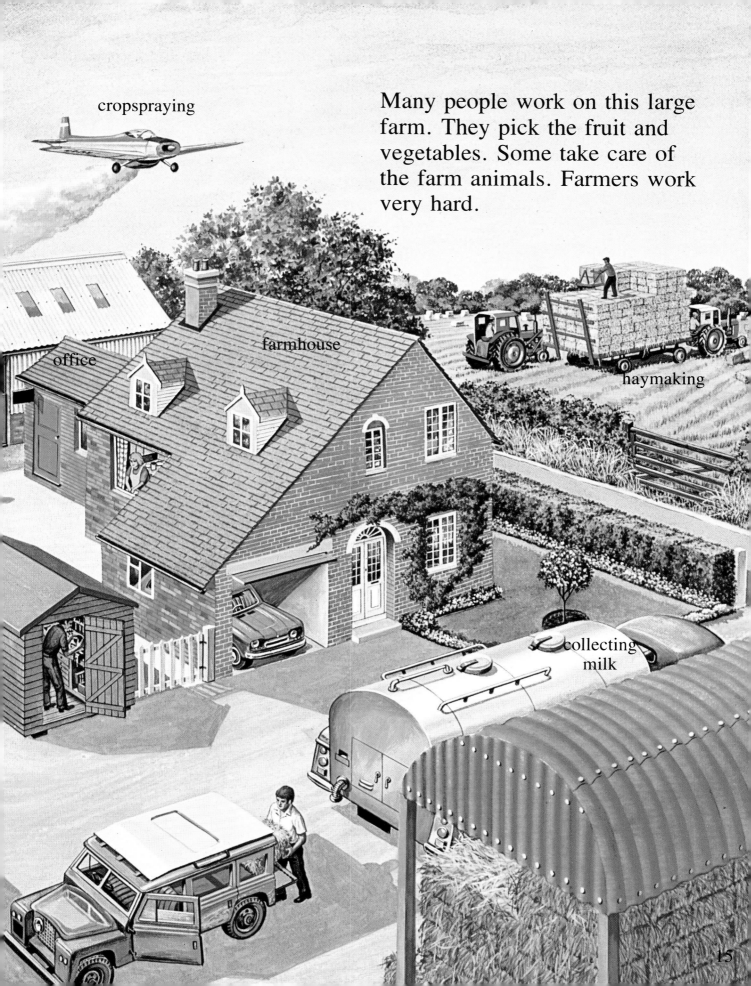

cropspraying

Many people work on this large farm. They pick the fruit and vegetables. Some take care of the farm animals. Farmers work very hard.

haymaking

office

farmhouse

collecting milk

15

Animal farming

Certain animals are very important to us. They provide us with things we need to live. Many animals provide meat. Cows also give milk and provide leather. Wool comes from sheep, and eggs come from chickens.

Animal farms are called ranches. Some cattle ranches are so big that ranchers use horses or jeeps to round up the cattle.

Oysters grow in shells under the water. On this oyster farm the oysters are being collected from "beds."

Different animals are raised in different parts of the world. People in Lapland use reindeer to pull sleds and give them milk. In Africa, ostriches are raised for their fine feathers. Llamas provide meat and wool in South America. Llama wool is very soft.

In winter, sheep grow thick coats of wool to keep warm. Sheep farmers dip the sheep in a special liquid to keep their coats clean and healthy.

Crop farming

Some farmers grow grain crops such as wheat and barley. Farmers use a tractor to plow their fields. The plow breaks up the soil for planting.

Next, the seeds are sown. A machine sprinkles the seeds in rows. Not all of the seeds will grow.

Some seeds will be eaten by birds. Some will die. So the farmer plants more than he will need. When the seeds begin to grow, small green plants appear. They need plenty of sun and rain to grow. Plants turn yellow when they are grown.

The picking of plants is called harvesting. Wheat and other grains are gathered with a combine harvester. This machine cuts down the plants and separates the grain from the stalks. The grain is put into sacks.

The stalks are used for straw. The grain is sent to mills. There, it is ground into flour, which is used for baking.

Gardening

Many people enjoy gardening for fun. They grow vegetables and flowers for their family. Some people look after gardens as a job. Gardeners plant flowers and take care of them. They decide what flowers to plant and where to plant them. Many gardeners work in parks. Others make gardens around homes.

Nurseries are places where plants and flowers are grown. Some plants are grown in glass houses called greenhouses. Plants can grow in a greenhouse even in winter. People buy plants from a nursery to put into their own gardens.

Working with trees

Trees are planted in places called tree plantations. Foresters plant the trees and look after them. Large trees are cut down with big chain saws. The trees are cut into lumber, which is used to make furniture and other goods.

WORKING AT SEA

Many people work at sea. Many jobs are done on boats. The big ship is a passenger liner. It takes people from one place to another. Fishers go out in trawlers to catch fish. Submarines can dive beneath the waves and travel underwater. In some jobs people stay at sea for a long time.

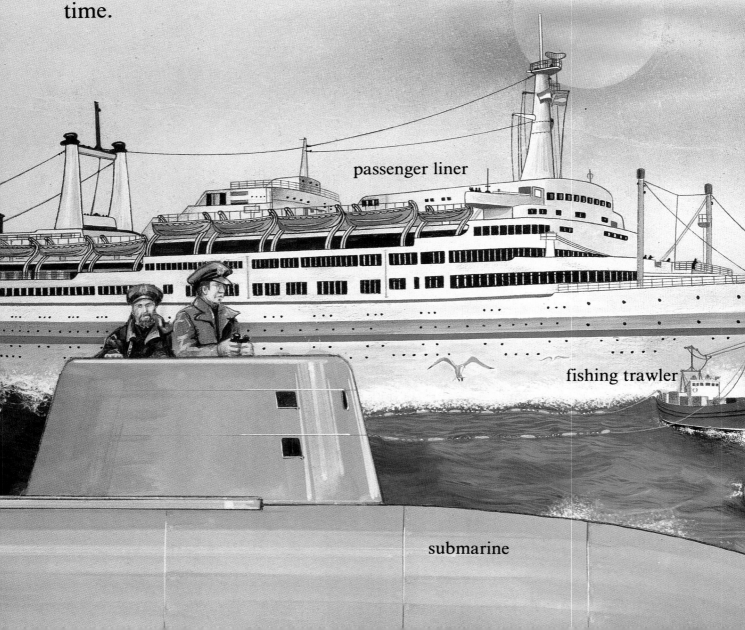

passenger liner

fishing trawler

submarine

People work at sea in other ways. They build rigs to drill for oil from the ocean bed. Astronauts sometimes land on the sea in their space capsules. Lighthouses warn of the danger of rocks. Helicopters sometimes rescue people from ships that are in trouble.

helicopter

oil rig

lighthouse

space capsule

lifeboat

70-001

Fishers

Most of the fish we eat come from the sea. Fishers go out in boats to catch them. The boats sometimes stay at sea for many days. The fishers below use a small boat. The big picture shows people fishing from shore. They use a net with floats along the top.

Fishers unload their fish at seaside towns. These towns are called fishing ports. Ports are often in sheltered bays with a harbor. The boats are safe there during rough weather.

Large fishing boats sail into the sea looking for fishing grounds. Fishers find a good place by looking for green water. Tiny animals called plankton make the water green. Fish eat plankton, so the fishers know they will find fish nearby.

The fishers drop large nets out of the boat. The nets spread out. Fish swim into them. Then the crew hauls the fish into the boat.

Have you ever eaten fish fresh from the sea? In some seaside towns, fishers catch fish and sell them the same day.

The merchant marine

People in the merchant marine work on ships that carry cargo or passengers. This ship is carrying cargo to another country. The cargo is stored in the front and middle of the ship. The crew works, eats, and sleeps on the ship. They may be at sea for many weeks before they reach a port.

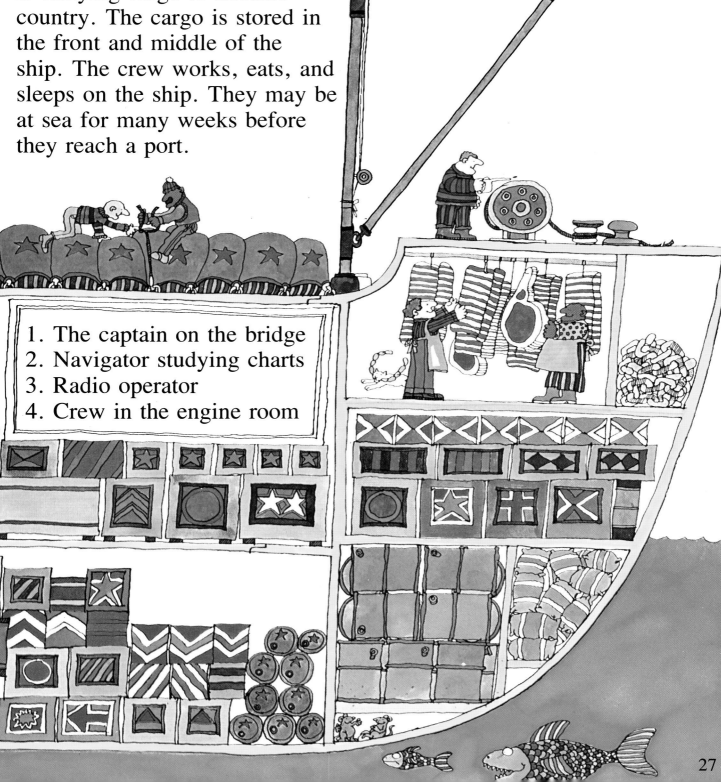

1. The captain on the bridge
2. Navigator studying charts
3. Radio operator
4. Crew in the engine room

The coast guard

Helicopters are sometimes used to help people at sea. Sick or injured people are pulled up into the helicopter. Then they are flown to a hospital.

Coast guard boats help people or ships in trouble at sea. Men and women join the coast guard just as they join the army or navy. The coast guard must be ready to go out to sea when a ship is in danger. The sea may be very rough when it goes out.

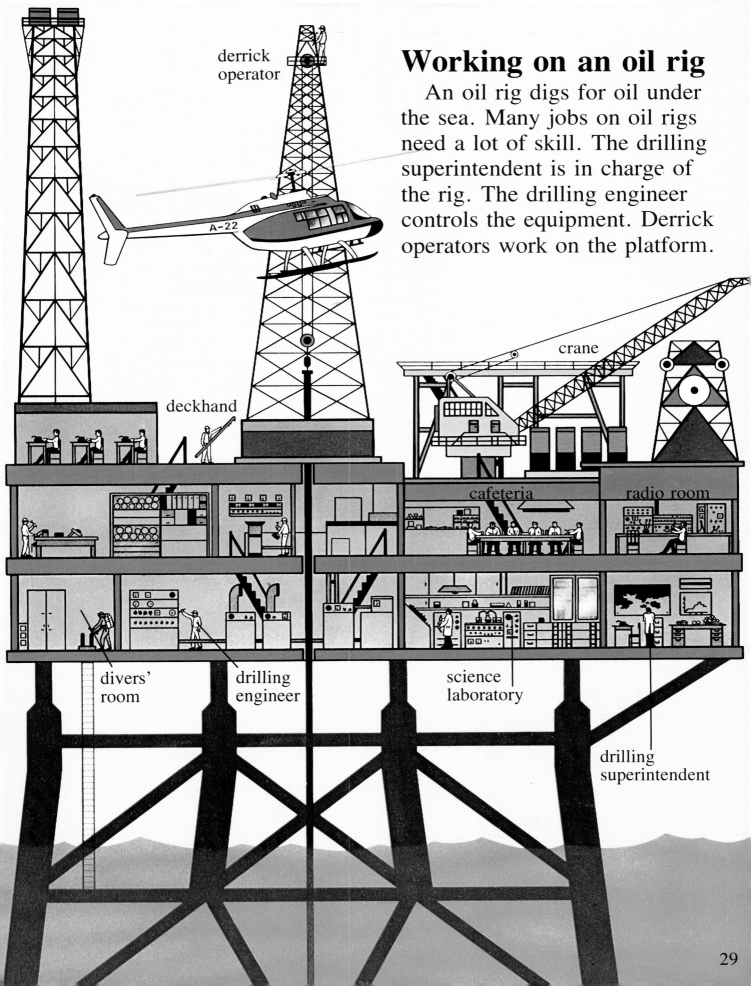

Working on an oil rig

An oil rig digs for oil under the sea. Many jobs on oil rigs need a lot of skill. The drilling superintendent is in charge of the rig. The drilling engineer controls the equipment. Derrick operators work on the platform.

derrick operator

deckhand

crane

cafeteria

radio room

divers' room

drilling engineer

science laboratory

drilling superintendent

Building and construction

Many people are needed to build a house. They all have different skills. First, someone chooses the land where the house will be built. Then an architect designs the house. Someone else orders materials to build with, such as wood.

A house needs walls, floors, a roof, doors and windows, and water and electricity. Each job needs people with different skills.

A surveyor uses special tools to measure the land where the house will be built. Surveyors must measure carefully.

The foundation of a house is built underground. People dig trenches and fill them with concrete to hold the house.

Bricklayers build the brick walls. Carpenters work on the wooden parts of the house, such as floors and doorways.

An architect designs the house.
Drawings are made to show
what the house will look like.
The drawings help other
workers.

The ground must be cleared
before work begins. A driver
uses a bulldozer to push the
ground and flatten it.

A plumber lays pipes for water.
An electrician puts in the wires
for electricity for lights and
other things.

Painters and decorators make
the house look nice. Painters
work both inside and outside.
Decorators work on the inside.

bricklayer

decorator

carpenter

plumber

The building site

Here you can see all the people working on a house. Bricklayers use cement to stick the bricks together. One man carries bricks to the bricklayer. A decorator is putting up wallpaper.

roof tiler

electrician

bulldozer

cement mixer

painter

surveyor

Engineers

Engineers work out the best way to make things. Some engineers make things that move, like airplanes, ships, cars, and rockets. Some engineers find ways to make machines work better or faster. Others work on ways to save fuel.

Civil engineers work at building things like roads and bridges. They make sure the right machines and materials are used. In the picture above, an engineer is studying the plans for a large office building.

In the big picture you can see some of the things engineers do. They build bridges, roads, buildings, and factories. It takes a lot of skill to plan these things. They must last for many years and be safe for the people who use them. Engineers also design machines.

These engineers are looking for natural gas. They must find it deep in the ground. They wear hard hats to protect their heads.

nurse

cafeteria

office manager

designing

supervisor

FACTORIES AND OFFICES

Working in a factory

Most of the things we use every day are made in factories. The factories are set up so that things can be made very quickly. This factory makes bicycles.

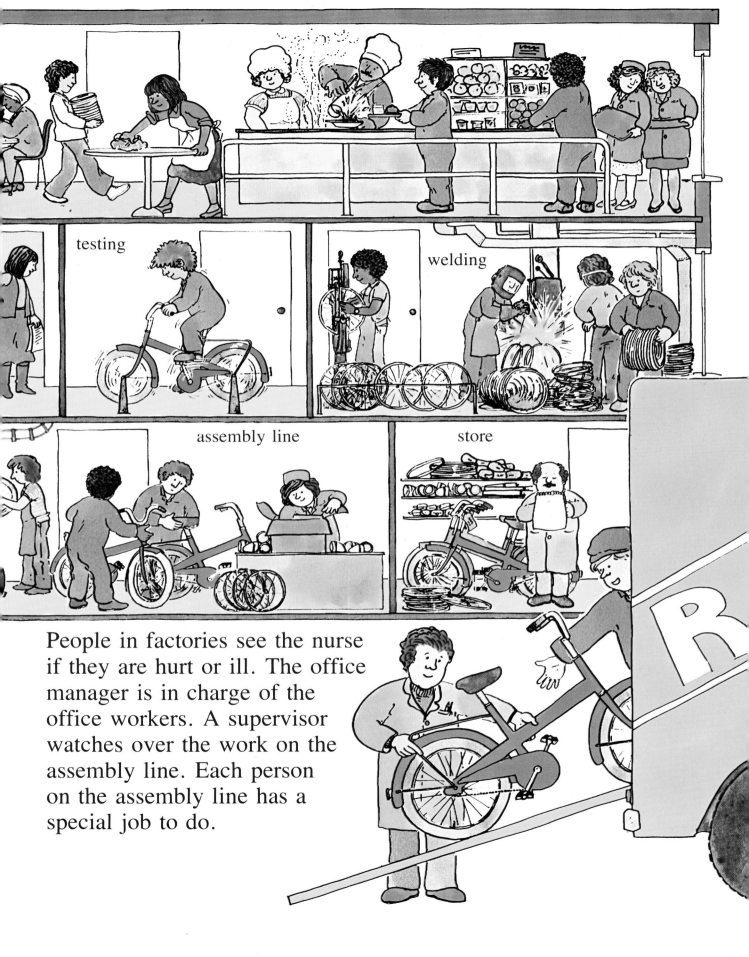

testing

welding

assembly line

store

People in factories see the nurse if they are hurt or ill. The office manager is in charge of the office workers. A supervisor watches over the work on the assembly line. Each person on the assembly line has a special job to do.

The assembly line

Cars are put together on assembly lines. They are not built one by one. They are passed along a line so that different parts of the car can be fit together. Jobs such as welding and drilling must be done hundreds of times each day. Some jobs are done by people, others by robots.

The car soon takes shape on the assembly line. One of the most important jobs to be done is the painting. Paint protects the metal from rust.

The worker in this German factory is using a machine to make ribbon. The ribbon will be used to decorate clothing.

Working with clothes

Clothes are made from many different kinds of material. Cotton comes from a plant. Wool comes from sheep. Some materials, such as nylon, are made from chemicals. The woman below is preparing silk in Thailand.

Designers draw patterns for the clothes. The material is then cut out. Pieces are sewn together with sewing machines. These women are making dresses.

Clothing is sold in stores. Workers in stores help people find clothes that fit and look nice.

Working in an office

This is an open-plan office. The boss has walls around her office. All the other people work in a big open space. A receptionist greets visitors and shows them where to go.

telephone operator

Secretaries type, answer phones, and file letters. A telephone operator switches calls to the right people by using a switchboard.

boss

receptionist

Start here

1

2

3

4 5 6 7

Bottom falls out of trash bag. Go back 1.

SERVICES

Some people perform services. They do not make or sell things. But they do jobs that are very important. All of the people in this game do jobs that help us in some way.

Collect pencil case from Lost and Found. Move on 3.

Hit librarian's books. Go back 6.

47 46 45 44 43 42 41 40 39 3

48

49

Hurt your arm. Go back 1.

Doctor fixes arm. Move on 3.

Taxi driver takes you home to Finish.

50 51 52 53 54 55 56 57 58

44

Drop pencil case. Go back 1.

Dog chases mail carrier. Go back 3.

Police officer helps you cross street to 24.

Correct sum for teacher. Extra throw.
7+2

Street sweeper finds case. Move on 3.

Bus driver won't wait. Miss 1 throw.

Home for snack.

You may see a mail carrier or a police officer on your way to school. When you get to school you will see your teacher. A librarian may help you find a book in the library. The doctor helps you when you are sick.

15 16 17 18 19 20 21
14 22
13 23
12 24
25
11 26
10 27
9 28
37 36 35 34 33 32 31 30 29
60 61 62 Finish

Dutch
police officer

English
police officer

Police officers

If you are ever lost, ask a police officer for help. Police officers patrol everywhere. Some walk in the streets. Others go in cars, motorcycles, or police boats. Sometimes police officers ride horses.

The police catch people who do something wrong, like stealing. They help out if there is an accident.

French
police
officer

This officer is directing traffic in India. The umbrella shades him from the hot sun. He stands on a platform so the drivers can see him better as they drive along.

Some roads get very busy during rush hours. Police helicopters fly over the cars. They warn drivers of traffic jams.

Police are there to answer your questions. They help you if you're in trouble.

Fire fighters

Fire fighters work from a fire house, where the fire engine is kept. They are always ready to act quickly to put out a fire. The fire fighters below are using a special foam to put out a fire.

Fire fighters do other jobs too. They help people who are stuck in elevators. They bring cats down from trees. Can you see the boy in the well? Fire fighters will rescue him.

Fire fighters have to train a lot before they are ready to go to fires. They practice using tall ladders. They must learn to use different kinds of equipment. Fire fighters not only put out fires. They help during floods too.

The postal service

People in the postal service see that letters and packages go to the right places. Some people collect letters. Others deliver them. What happens when you mail a letter or a package?

A mail carrier collects all the letters and packages and takes them to a sorting office.

The letters must be sorted so that they go to the right towns. Machines help do this.

Mail goes to different towns by train, truck, or airplane.

In the post office, letters are sorted again. They are sorted by neighborhood and address.

Mail carriers collect the mail from the post office. They bring it to your house.

Trash collectors

Trash collectors take away trash from the streets and from our homes. They go to all the houses and pick up the garbage. They use big trucks.

The truck takes the trash to a dump. These dumps are usually outside a town. There, the trash is often burned. Trash collectors start work early in the morning.

Teachers

Teachers in elementary schools teach all subjects. Those in high schools often teach only one subject. They need to know all about their subject so they can help children to learn.

The class on the right is in Sri Lanka. The weather is hot there. The teacher can teach some lessons outside.

Some teachers teach subjects like sports, music, and dancing. These children are playing a game in North Africa.

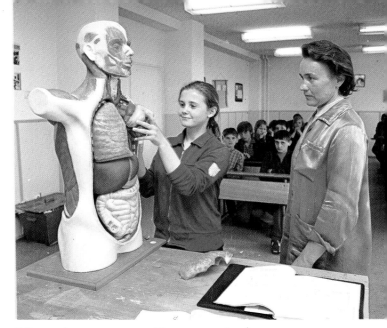

Teachers usually work in a classroom. This lesson is about how the body works. The teacher is using a model to show the different parts of the body. The children can see parts inside the body.

Librarians

A library is a place where people can go to borrow books. You can study in a library too. You can use different books in the library without having to take them home.

Librarians look after a library. They keep a record of everyone who borrows books. They know a lot about books and can answer your questions.

Working in a hospital

Sick people sometimes have to go to a hospital. People who work in hospitals know how to help sick people get better. Doctors and nurses work in a hospital. Other people work there too.

This boy has hurt his leg. A man is giving him first aid. He keeps the boy still so that he will not hurt himself more.

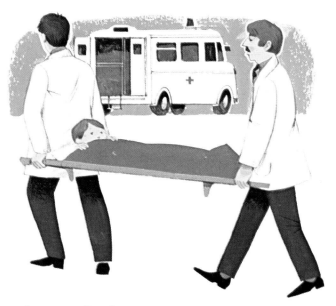

An ambulance comes to take the boy to a hospital. The boy is carried on a stretcher so that he will keep his leg still.

At the hospital, a doctor examines the boy. She finds that the boy's leg is broken.

The boy cannot walk on his broken leg. A hospital helper pushes the boy in a wheelchair.

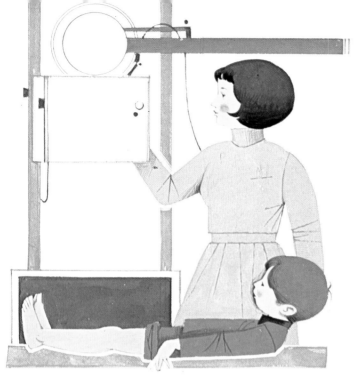

A special hospital worker takes an X-ray picture of the boy's leg. An X-ray picture shows the inside of the body. It will show how the bone is broken.

The doctor puts the leg into a plaster cast. This will keep the boy's leg straight until the bone mends.

After a few days, the boy can begin to move about. He uses crutches to walk with. People in the hospital help him.

While he is in the hospital, the boy is looked after by nurses. They bring him meals and see that he is comfortable.

Doctors

In some parts of the world, towns are far apart. A doctor may be far away. This doctor uses an airplane to get to people who need help.

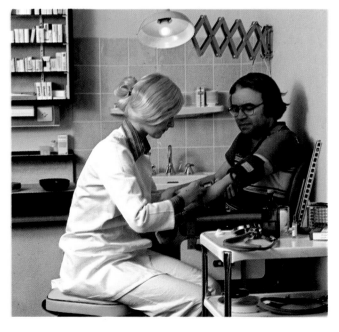

Not all doctors work in a hospital. Some doctors see people in their offices or at a clinic. People who are not badly ill can be treated there.

Doctors find out what is wrong with people. They tell people what medicine to take to get well. Sometimes doctors give people shots. A shot may keep you from getting sick.

Nurses

Nurses usually work in hospitals. They help doctors. They look after people who are sick in bed. They give people medicines and serve them meals. Nurses go to special schools to learn how to help sick people.

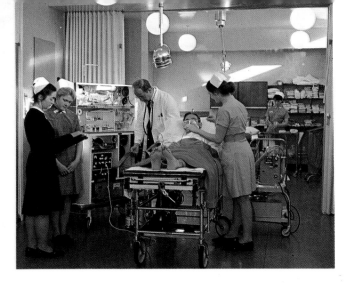

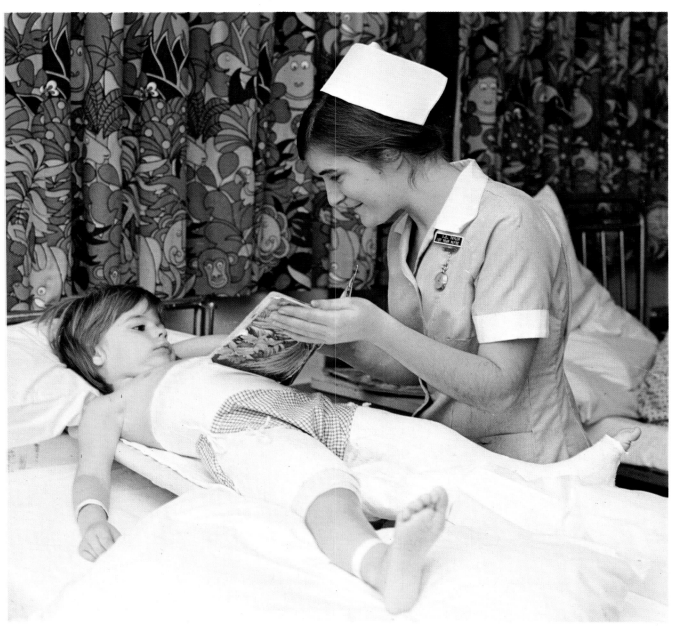

Scientists

Scientists try to find out more about the way things work and why they happen. Some scientists try to find new medicines or new types of food. Others study the past. Some scientists study how people lived a long time ago.

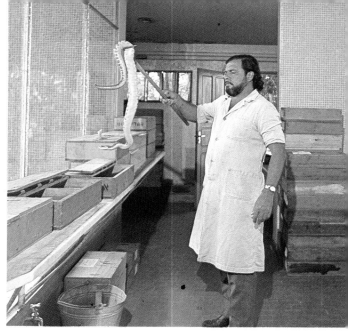

Scientists sometimes use animals to find out about new medicines. The scientist at the left is using a snake.

Some scientists dig into the earth to find things left by people of long ago. This group is digging up an old city.

This scientist is in a laboratory. She is studying what happens when certain chemicals are mixed together.

Scientists study the weather. They use special tools to measure winds and rainfall.

Working with money

Everyone needs money. Without money you cannot buy the things you need to live. Money can be in paper bills or coins. It is made in a place called the mint. The mint makes all the money in a country. No one else is allowed to make it.

New money is taken to a bank. Guards use an armored truck to keep the money safe from robbers.

Many people keep some of the money they earn in a bank. The bank keeps the money safe until people want it. Cashiers in a bank take in and give out money to people who have a bank account.

People pay for things they buy in a store. The storekeeper puts the money into a cash register.

At the end of the day, the storekeeper counts up all the money in the cash register. This storekeeper will take the money he has earned to a bank.

The storekeeper gives the money to a cashier. The cashier counts it and writes down the amount.

Working on a newspaper

Working on a newspaper is a very busy job. Newspapers are often printed every day. They must have all the latest news in them. The editor is in charge of the paper. Reporters find out news and write stories.

People call the newspaper if something interesting happens.

The editor sends a reporter to find out more.

The reporter phones in the story. A typist types it out.

The editor decides how much space to give the story. An important story will be on the front page of the newspaper.

Stories are keyed into a computer and made into print.

An editor reads and corrects the first copies, called proofs.

The stories are arranged in pages. The paper is printed.

Newspapers are delivered all over the city by trucks.

People can buy newspapers at stands all over town.

Newspapers in cities and many towns come out every day. Some small town newspapers come out only once a week. Some cities have small neighborhood newspapers. These often come out once a week. People who work on a weekly newspaper do not have to work so fast.

GLOSSARY

These words are defined the way they are used in the book.

ambulance (AM byuh luhns) a vehicle that carries sick or hurt people

architect (AHR kuh tekt) a person who plans buildings

assembly line (uh SEM blee lyn) a place where people put together one object out of many parts

baker (BAY kuhr) a person who cooks bread and cakes

barber (BAHR buhr) a person who cuts men's hair

boss (bahs) a person who gives orders to other workers

bricklayer (BRIHK lay uhr) a person who builds with bricks

butcher (BUCH uhr) a person who sells meat

cargo (KAHR goh) things that are carried in a ship or truck to be sold

cashier (kash EER) someone who has charge of money

carpenter (KAHR puhn tuhr) someone who builds with wood

cash register (kash rehj ih stuhr) a machine that holds money

combine harvester (KAHM byn HAHR vuhs tuhr) a machine that collects and cleans grain

decorator (DEHK uh rayt uhr) a person who makes the insides of houses look nice

department store (dih PAHRT muhnt stohr) a store with different places for selling different things

derrick operator (DEHR ihk awp uhr ayt uhr) a person who works derricks, which are tall buildings holding machines for oil wells

design (dih ZYN) to plan something

dough (doh) a soft mass of flour that can be cooked to make bread

editor (EHD uht uhr) a person who checks over the work of writers

electrician (ih lehk TRIHSH uhn) a person who works with electrical wires and devices

electricity (ih lehk TRIHS uht ee) a kind of energy

elevator (EHL uh vayt uhr) a small room that can go up and down to carry people and things from one floor to another

engine (EHN juhn) a machine that is used to run something, such as a car or airplane

engineer (ehn juh NEER) a person who figures out how to build things or how to make things work

factory (FAK tuh ree) a place where things are made

foundation (fown DAY shuhn) the support on which a building stands

furniture (FUHR nih chuhr) things such as chairs and tables that are used in a room

gardener (GAHRD uh nuhr) a person who takes care of growing plants

grain (grayn) food that comes from grasses such as wheat or corn

greenhouse (GREEN hous) a glass house for growing plants

hairdresser (HAYR drehs uhr) a person who cuts a woman's hair

helicopter (HEHL uh kahp tuhr) an aircraft that stays in the air using spinning propellers

librarian (ly BREHR ee uhn) a person who is in charge of a library

llama (LAH muh) a hoofed animal of South America

mail carrier (MAYL cayr ee uhr) a person who picks up and delivers letters and packages

manager (MAN ih juhr) a person who makes decisions about a job

medicine (MEHD uh suhn) something that is used to treat sickness

merchant marine (MUHR chuhnt muh REEN) trading ships and people who sail them

mint (mihnt) a place where metal is made into money

motorcycle (MOHT uhr sy kuhl) a machine like a bicycle driven by an engine

newspaper (NOOZ pay puhr) a paper that is made and sent out regularly and has news and stories

nursery (NUHR suh ree) a place where trees and plants are grown

office (AWF uhs) a place in a building where people work

oil rig (OYL rihg) a building that holds machines for getting oil

ostrich (AHS trihch) a large African bird that cannot fly

oyster (OIS tuhr) a soft shellfish with a two-part shell

passenger liner (PAS uhn juhr LY nuhr) a large boat that takes people across the sea

plankton (PLANG tuhn) tiny

animals and plants that live in the water

plumber (PLUHM uhr) a person who puts in and fixes water pipes and equipment

police officer (puh LEES awf uh suhr) a person who keeps order and makes sure the law is followed

provide (pruh VYD) to give out

receptionist (rih SEHP shuh nuhst) a person who greets visitors at an office

reindeer (RAYN deer) a large deer with antlers that lives in northern countries

reporter (rih POHRT uhr) a person who finds out what is happening and writes about it in a newspaper

scientist (SY uhn tuhst) a person who does work in science

secretary (SEHK ruh tair ee) a person who handles letters and papers in an office

shoemaker (SHOO may kuhr) a person who makes or fixes shoes

superintendent (soo phur ihn TEHN duhnt) a person who is in charge of a job

supermarket (SOO puhr MAHR kuht) a large store where many kinds of food and goods are sold

surveyor (suhr VAY uhr) a person who measures land and makes plans for building on it

telephone operator (TEHL uh fohn awp uhr ay tuhr) a person who answers and uses a telephone system

tractor (TRAK tuhr) a large vehicle that is used on farms

trash collector (trash kuh LEHK tuhr) a person who takes trash to a central dump

trawler (TRAW luhr) a special boat used for fishing with big nets

typesetter (TYP seht uhr) a person who works a machine to type out the words in books and newspapers

vegetable (VEHJ uht uh buhl) food that comes from plants

X-ray (EHKS ray) a way of taking a picture of the inside of the body

yeast (yeest) a substance made of tiny plants. It is used to make bread rise.

FURTHER READING

Ancona, George. *And What Do You Do?: A Book About People and Their Work.* New York: Dutton, 1976. 47pp.

Bellville, Cheryl Walsh. *Farming Today, Yesterday's Way.* Minneapolis: Carolrhoda Books, 1984.

Butterworth, William E. *Careers in the Services: Opportunities From Mechanics to Medicine.* New York: F. Watts, 1976. 72pp.

Criner, Beatrice H. *Jobs in Personal Services.* New York: Lothrop, Lee and Shepard Company, 1974. 95pp.

Criner, Beatrice H. *Jobs in Public Service.* New York: Lothrop, Lee and Shepard Company, 1974. 96pp.

Fradin, Dennis B. *Farming.* Chicago: Childrens Press, 1983.

Greene, Laura. *Careers in the Computer Industry.* New York: F. Watts, 1983.

Hankin, Rebecca. *I Can Be a Musician.* Chicago: Childrens Press, 1984.

Horton, Louise. *Careers in Office Work.* New York: F. Watts, 1977. 66pp.

Horton, Louise. *Careers in Theatre, Music and Dance.* New York: F. Watts, 1976. 61pp.

Lee, Essie E. *Careers in the Health Field.* New York: Messner, 1972. 191pp.

Martini, Terri. *Cowboys.* Chicago: Childrens Press, 1981.

McHugh, Mary. *Careers in Engineering and Engineering Technology.* New York: F. Watts, 1978. 66pp.

Olesky, Walter. *Careers in the Animal*

Kingdom. New York: Messner, 1980.

Ramos, Gloria. *Careers in Construction*. Minneapolis: Lerner Publications Company, 1975. 36pp.

Ray, Jo Anne. *Careers with a Police Department*. Minneapolis: Lerner Publications Company, 1973. 36pp.

Reuter, Margaret. *Careers in a Police Department*. Milwaukee: Raintree Publishers, 1977. 48pp.

Rockwell, Anne L. *When We Grow Up*. New York: Dutton, 1981.

Rosenfeld, Megan. *Careers in Journalism for the New Woman*. New York: F. Watts, 1977. 116pp.

Seed, Suzanne. *Saturday's Child: 36 Women Talk About Their Jobs*. Chicago: J. P. O'Hara, 1973. 159pp.

Sobol, Harriet L. *Pete's House*. New York: Macmillan, 1978. 58pp.

Stashower, Gloria. *Careers in Management for the New Woman*. New York: F. Watts, 1978. 120pp.

Vandervoort, Thomas J. *Sailing is for Me*. Minneapolis: Lerner Publications, 1981.

Wakin, Edward. *Jobs in Communications*. New York: Lothrop, Lee and Shepard Company, 1974. 96pp.

Walker, Les. *Housebuilding for Children*. New York: Overlook Press, 1977. 174pp.

QUESTIONS TO THINK ABOUT

Working in Shops

Do you remember?

What is a shopping area?

Where is most bread made today?

What does a baker use to make bread?

What are some of the things a hairdresser does?

Where are most shoes made? What does a shoemaker do?

What are some of the jobs people do in a department store?

Find out about . . .

Shopping areas. Is there a shopping area near your neighborhood? Where does your family shop? What different kinds of stores are there?

Bakers. How many different things can you name that are made by bakers? Where would you find the directions for making a cake? Give the directions for making a kind of cake you like.

Stores and shops. Name some stores or shops you did not read about in this book. Who works there?

Working on the Land

Do you remember?

What are some of the animals farmers raise?

What are some of the things farmers grow?

What are llamas used for? Where are they raised?

Why does a farmer plow a field?

What is wheat used for?

What is a greenhouse?

What do foresters do?

Find out about . . .

Grain farmers. Where is most wheat grown in this country? How large are some of the wheat farms? What are some other grains that farmers grow? What kind of machines do these farmers use?

Animal farming. What animals besides cows and sheep do farmers raise? What are these animals used for?

Gardening. Where can gardeners work in your town? What kinds of things can they do?

Working At Sea

Do you remember?

What are lighthouses used for?

What do fishers catch fish in?

What is a port?

What is the merchant marine? What are some of the jobs done by people in the merchant marine?

What does the Coast Guard do?

Who are some of the people who work on an oil rig?

Find out about . . .

Passenger liners. Why do people travel by passenger liner? What are some of the jobs people do on a liner?

Fishers. What skills are needed by people who fish for a living? What is life on a fishing boat like?

The Coast Guard. Who can join the Coast Guard? What are some of the things a person in the Coast Guard would do?

Oil rigs. Why do people dig for oil under the sea? Where are oil rigs found in this country? How many people work on a rig?

Building and Construction

Do you remember?

What does an architect do?

What do carpenters do?

Why are so many different kinds of workers needed to build a house?

What are some of the things engineers do?

Find out about . . .

Building trades. Name some of the people who

work at building houses. What does each one do? What kind of school or other training does each one need?

Engineers. What are some of the different kinds of engineers? What training do engineers need? Where can they get their training?

A famous builder. John A. Roebling designed and built many famous bridges. Find out more about his life and the bridges he built.

Road building. Who are some of the people who work at building roads and streets?

Factories and Offices

Do you remember?

Who are some of the people who work in a factory?

What does an assembly line supervisor do?

What are some of the different jobs done on an assembly line?

What are three different kinds of cloth? What is used to make each one?

What do clothes designers do?

Name three kinds of office workers.

Are all bosses men?

Find out about . . .

Factory jobs. What are some factories in your

town or state? What things are made there? What are some of the jobs people do in these factories?

The assembly line. Why do factories use an assembly line? What did Henry Ford have to do with the assembly line?

Office workers. Name some office workers. What skills do these people need? Where can they get training in these skills?

Services

Do you remember?

Name at least six different kinds of service workers.

What are some of the things police officers do?

Why do some police departments have helicopters?

What do fire fighters do besides put out fires?

What does the postal service do?

How does mail get from one town to another?

Who brings letters to your home?

What do trash collectors do with the garbage they pick up?

How are high school teachers different from elementary teachers?

Who takes care of a library?

What will a doctor do if you break your leg?

Why do doctors give people shots?

What do nurses do?

What are some things scientists study?

Why do some scientists dig into the earth?

Where is money made?

Where can people put their money to keep it safe?

Name some of the jobs at a newspaper.

Find out about . . .

City workers. Police officers and fire fighters usually work for a town or city. Who are some other people who work for a town or city? What services do they perform?

Police and fire departments. Who can become a police officer? Who can become a fire fighter? How much schooling must these people have? What other training do they need?

The postal service. Where is the post office nearest your home? What are some of the things you can get done at a post office?

Teachers. How long does it take to become a teacher? How much schooling must a teacher have? What are some good things about being a teacher?

Hospitals. What hospital is nearest your home?

What are some of the different kinds of jobs done at a hospital? Which do you think you would like best? What training would you need before you could do this job?

Salaries. People are paid salaries for doing work. What kind of jobs pay good salaries? What are some of the things you could do to make sure you got a job that paid a good salary?

Selling. Many people sell things for a living. Find out more about selling jobs. What are some different kinds of jobs in selling?

PROJECTS

Project — Neighborhood Helpers

Make a list of all the people who work in your neighborhood. Write down what they do. You might see a police officer or a mail carrier. Or you might see people fixing your street or working on electrical wires. Make a list showing what they do and what special clothes they may wear.

Project — My Career

Pretend you are 25 years old. Write a short story telling what your job is. Tell about the kinds of things you do each day. Also, tell what special things you have to know to do that job.

INDEX

Ambulance 54
Animal farming 14, 16-17
Architect 30, 31
Assembly line 38-39
Baker 7, 8-9
Bank 60, 61
Barber 10
Bricklayer 31
Butcher 7
Carpenter 30
Cashier 60-61
Clothes designer 40
Coast guard 28
Crop farming 14-15, 18-19
Decorator 31
Doctor 45, 54-55, 56
Editor 62
Electrician 31
Engineer 34, 35
Factory 8, 36-41
Farmer 14-15. 18
Fire fighter 48-49
Fisher 22, 24-45
Forester 21
Gardening 20-21
Harvesting 19
Hairdresser 10-11
Hospital 54-55, 56, 57
Librarian 45, 53
Mail carrier 44, 50

Merchant marine 26-27
Newspaper 62-63
Nurse 55, 57
Office 42-43
Oil rig 23, 29
Plumber 31
Police officer 46-47
Receptionist 42, 43
Reporter 62
Scientist 58-59
Secretary 43
Shoemakeer 11
Supermarket 12-13
Surveyor 30
Teacher 45, 52-53
Trash collector 51

Photo Credits: Heather Angel, M.Sc. F.R.P.S.; Australian News and Information Baureau; British Tourist Authority; Forestry Commission; Robert Harding Associates; Illustrated London News; Cees van der Meulen; New Civil Engineer; Pace Photography; John Parker; Picturepoint; Vidal Sassoon/ Richard Lohr; Sutton Seeds; Toyota (U.K. Ltd.); United Kingdom Atomic Energy Authority; Thomas A. Wilkie Company; ZEFA.

Front cover: Mark Snyder.

Illustrators: Fred Anderson; Geoffrey Burns; Richard Eastland; Philip Emms; Dan Escott; John Fraser; Elizabeth Graham-Yool; Richard Hook; Eric Jewell; Ben Manchipp; Angus McBride; John Sibbick.